FORT WORTH
W9-BZC-037
9413

Native American Biographies

Chief John Ross

Rachel A. Koestler-Grack

Heinemann Library
Chicago, Illinois

Customer Service 888–454–2279

Visit our website at www.heinemannlibrary.com

Designed by Kim Saar/Heinemann Library
Maps by John Fleck
Photo research by Alan Gottlieb
Printed in China by WKT Company Limited

08 07 06 05 04
10 9 8 7 6 5 4 3 2 1

Library of Congress Cataloging-in-Publication Data
Koestler-Grack, Rachel A., 1973-
Chief John Ross / Rachel A. Koestler-Grack.
p. cm. -- (Native American biographies)
Summary: A biography of John Ross, principal chief of the Cherokee people on the Trail of Tears, describing his childhood, leadership of his people, struggles with the United States government, and the split of the Cherokee Nation.
Includes bibliographical references and index.
ISBN 1-4034-5000-5 (lib. bdg.) -- ISBN 1-4034-5007-2 (pbk.)
1. Ross, John, 1790-1866--Juvenile literature. 2. Cherokee Indians--Kings and rulers--Biography--Juvenile literature. 3. Cherokee Indians--Government relations--Juvenile literature. 4. Cherokee Indians--Relocation--Oklahoma--Juvenile literature. 5. Trail of Tears, 1838--Juvenile literature. [1. Ross, John, 1790-1866. 2. Cherokee Indians--Biography. 3. Indians of North America--Biography. 4. Kings, queens, rulers, etc. 5. Trail of Tears, 1838.] I. Title. II. Series: Native American biographies (Heinemann Library (Firm))
E99.C5R6744 2004
975.004'97557'0092--dc22

2003020490

Acknowledgments
The author and publisher are grateful to the following for permission to reproduce copyright material:
p. 4 Library of Congress/Neg.# LC-USZC4-3156; p. 5 Dorothy Sullivan/Memory Circle Studios; p. 6 National Archives/Neg # NWDNS-III-B-547; p. 7 Collection of the New York Historical Society; p. 9 National Anthropological Archives/Smithsonian Institution/Neg.#NAA-1044-b; p. 11 Marilyn "Angel" Wynn/NativeStock; p. 12 Courtesy Roane County Heritage Commission; p. 13 Library of Congress/Neg.#LC-USZ6-858; p. 15 Eastern National; pp. 16, 21 National Portrait Gallery/Smithsonian Institution/Art Resource, NY; pp. 18, 26, 27 Gilcrease Museum; p. 19 Courtesy of Chief Vann House Historic Site; p. 20 Courtesy Georgia Division of Archives and History/Office of Secretary of State; p. 22 Rare books and Manuscripts Division/New York Public Library/Astor Lenox and Tilden Foundations; p. 23 National Archives/Neg.#RCD05964; p. 25 Oklahoma Historical Society; p. 28 Cherokee Nation; p. 29 Lisa LaRue/ Cherokee Nation Cultural Resource Center

Cover photographs by (foreground) Philbrook Museum of Art/Tulsa Oklahoma, (background) Corbis

Special thanks to Lisa LaRue for her help in the preparation of this book.

The image of Chief John Ross on the cover of this book was painted in 1848 by John Neagle.
The background shows a mountain range in the eastern United States.

Contents

Some words are shown in bold, **like this.** You can find out what they mean by looking in the glossary.

Finding Courage

On October 1, 1838, John Ross climbed onto his horse. He prepared to lead the Cherokee people on a long journey. Only months before John found out that the Cherokees had to leave their **homeland.** United States soldiers forced them to move west. Winter came early that year. Cold winds blew and snow covered the ground. The people did not have enough blankets and clothing. Many walked over the frozen ground without shoes.

This image of John Ross was painted around 1835.

Each day, John found food and water for weak travelers. His wife, Quatie, gave her only blanket to a sick child. A few days later, Quatie became sick and died. More than 4,000 Cherokees died because of the trip. Cherokees called their journey *Nunna-da-ul-tsun-yi.* In English it is known as the Trail of Tears. Despite his sorrows, John Ross found the courage to lead his people to their new home. He never let them down.

Some Cherokees tried to stop the United States government from taking their homes.

Little John

John Ross was born on October 3, 1790, in Turkeytown. This town was near the Coosa River in the southeastern corner of present-day Alabama. John was the third of nine children. His mother was a part-Cherokee woman named Mollie McDonald. His father was Daniel Ross, a Scottish **immigrant.** Daniel came to America from Scotland. After Daniel married Mollie, they lived with the Cherokee people.

John Ross lived in this house in present-day Georgia when he was about twenty years old.

This painting of two Cherokees was made by George Catlin. It shows what Cherokees dressed like in the early 1800s.

Later John's family moved from Turkeytown to a place by the Tennessee River. This area is now Chattanooga, Tennessee. There, John's father opened a **trading post** called Ross's **Landing.** As a boy, John often helped at the trading post. He would stack furs and deerskins on tables. Daniel sometimes rewarded John's hard work with a peppermint drop from the candy jar.

John was proud of his Cherokee **heritage.** One time John's grandmother dressed him in **settlers'** clothes and sent him out to play. John's friends laughed. John burst into tears and ran back into the house. "I want to dress like a Cherokee," he told his grandmother. So she dressed him in **buckskin.** He smiled and skipped out to play.

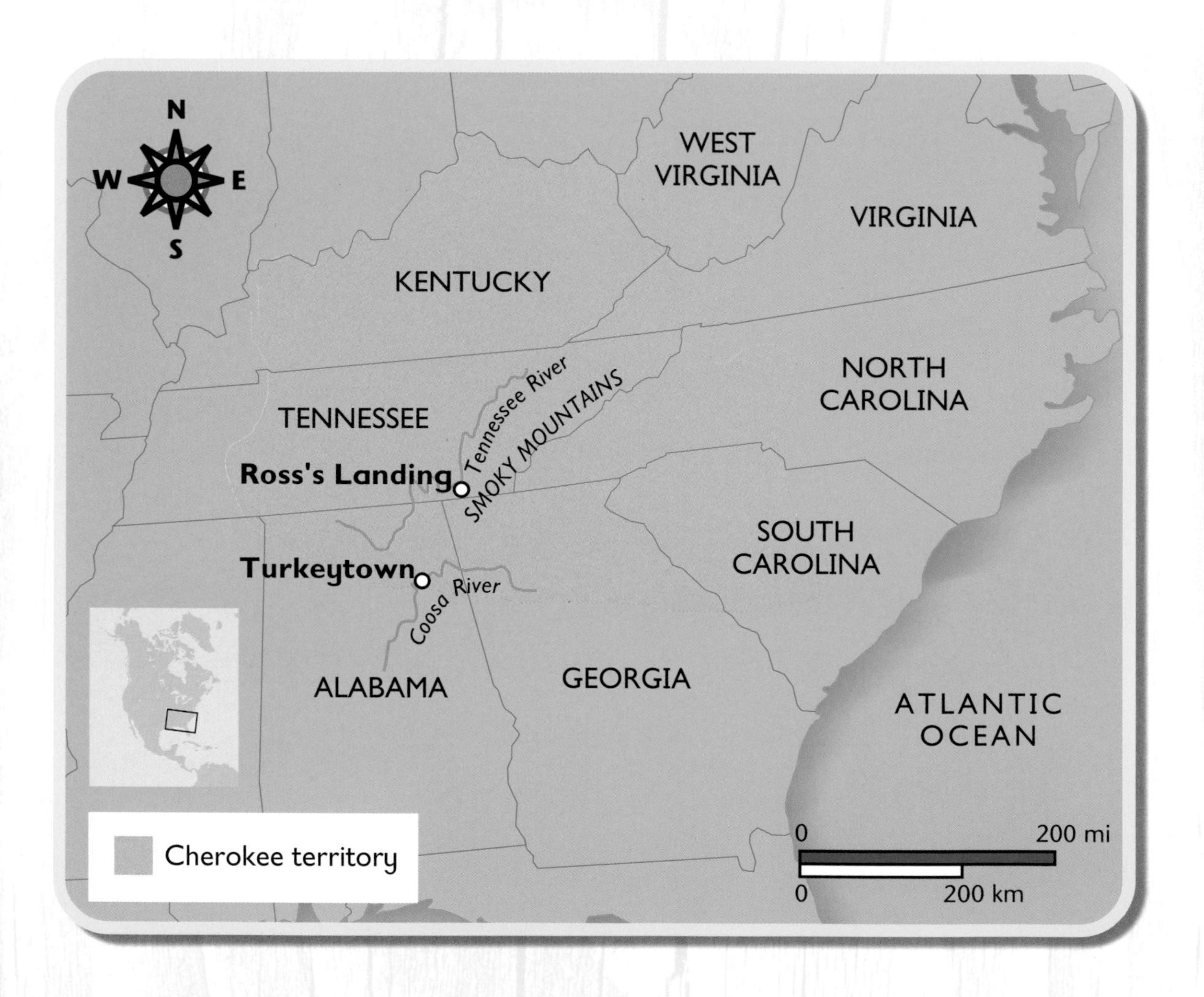

Cherokee men and boys have played stickball for hundreds of years. This photograph was taken in 1888.

John's father built a schoolhouse near their home. He hired a **tutor** to teach his children. John studied hard at school. After school he and his friends raced horses, explored the forests, and fished in nearby streams. John was a fast runner and an excellent student. His hard work won the respect of his friends. They looked up to John as a leader.

A Special Event

When John was seven, he took part in the Festival of the Green Corn. During this **ceremony,** John was accepted as an adult among his people. On the first day, John **fasted** with the other Cherokee men. This helped him concentrate on the ceremony. The second day John ate bitter **herbs** to **purify** his body. On the third day, the men drank a strong liquid. John also drank a cup of the powerful drink.

Cherokee Stories

Many Cherokee stories were about the Raven **Mocker.** In Cherokee stories, this invisible bird is a bad witch. The Raven Mocker comes to steal the lives of sick people. Only a **medicine man** can keep the Raven Mocker away.

On the evening of the third day, the people gathered for a feast. They ate deer meat, fresh bread, and roasted corn. After the meal people danced around the fires. When night came, John and the other boys gathered around the **elders** to hear stories.

These present-day Cherokees are taking part in the Green Corn Dance.

A few days later, Daniel told John that he would be going to a private school in Kingston, Tennessee. John was sad to move away from home. At the school, John studied hard and got good grades. When he left the school, John took a job with a local trading business. But in 1808 John reccived some sad news. His mother had died. He returned home for her burial.

John went to a private school like this one in Kingston, Tennessee.

Timeline

1797	1808	1809
John took part in the Festival of the Green Corn	Mollie Ross died	John kept peace between the Western Cherokees and settlers

A year later John took a job with United States government leaders. They asked John to keep peace between a group of Cherokees and nearby **settlers.** John was well liked by both the settlers and the Cherokees. His trip was a success. John believed that Cherokees and settlers could live peacefully together. He trusted that the government leaders would keep their word. He did not ever imagine that things could change.

United States Indian Agent Return J. Meigs sent John Ross on a mission to help a group of Cherokees live together with settlers.

Fighting the Red Sticks

In 1813 a group of Creek Indians called Red Sticks attacked Fort Mims in present-day Alabama. This was the beginning of the Creek War. A man named Andrew Jackson led the United States Army against the Red Sticks. Jackson asked the Cherokees to help. The Red Sticks were enemies of the Cherokees. Cherokee leaders sent 800 **warriors** to fight at the Battle of Horseshoe Bend. There John Ross and his warriors attacked the Red Sticks from behind.

In Their Own Words

After the Battle of Horseshoe Bend, John Ross wrote down a speech for Andrew Jackson. Jackson said the battle was "one of the greatest victories of the American frontier." These words became very famous.

While the Red Sticks turned to fight the Cherokees, United States soldiers attacked the Red Sticks from the front. More than 1,000 Red Stick Indians died in the Battle of Horseshoe Bend. Only 50 United States soldiers and Cherokee warriors were killed.

This is where the Battle of Horseshoe Bend took place. The battlefield is now a national military park located near present-day Daviston, Alabama.

John Ross was 51 years old when this picture was painted.

The Cherokee **warriors** returned home to a horrible shock. While they were away, United States soldiers had destroyed their villages. The soldiers had stolen their horses, killed cattle and hogs, and taken corn. Even worse, the Cherokee people lost a huge area of their **homeland.** John was very angry. Fourteen years earlier, the United States government had promised the Cherokees that they could always keep their land. Now the government refused to give the land back.

On September 14, 1816, John and other Cherokee leaders signed the **Treaty** of Turkeytown. In this agreement the Cherokees gave up some of their land. After the Treaty of Turkeytown, John realized that government leaders might not keep their promises. John wanted to protect the rights of his people.

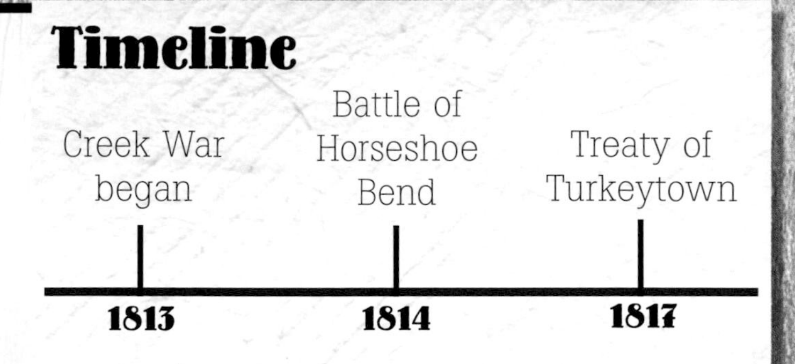

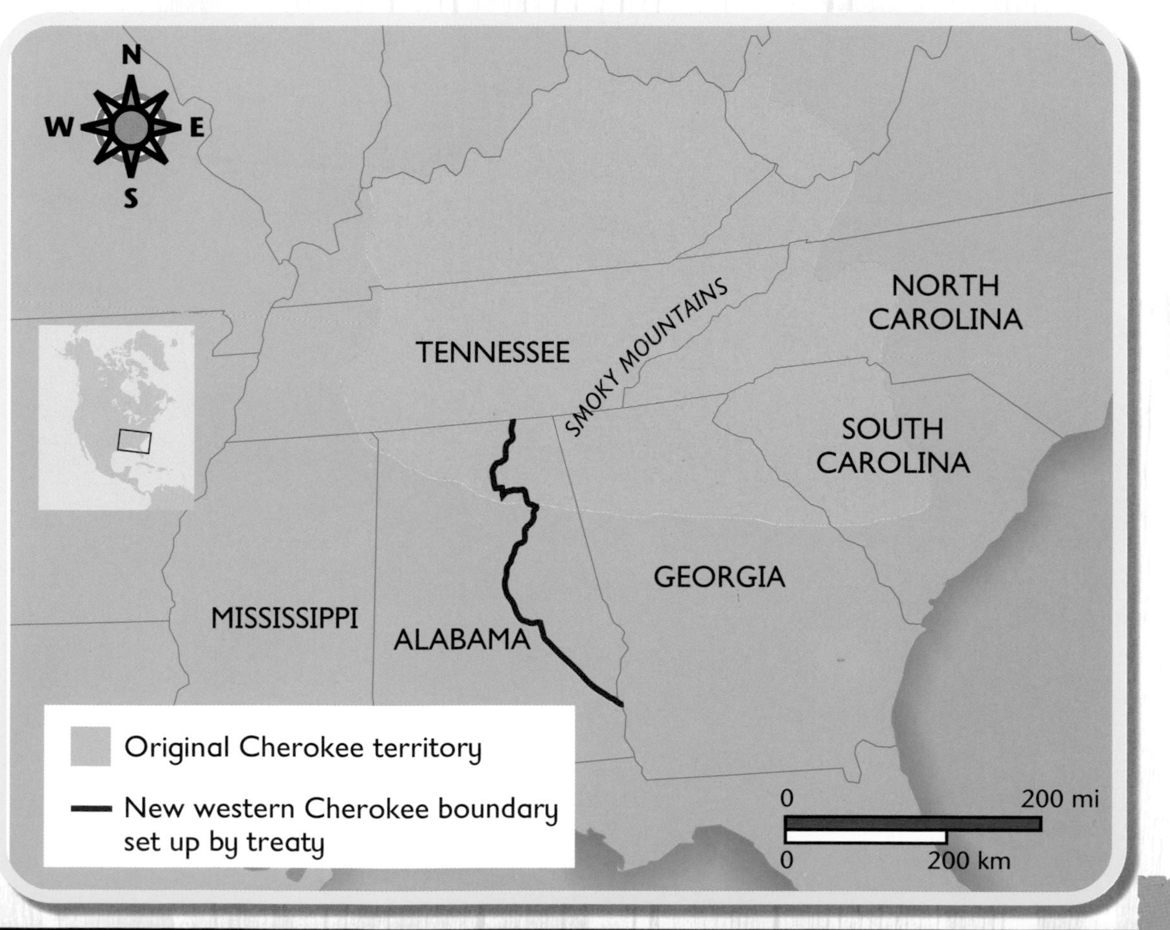

Principal Chief

Shortly after the Creek War, John married Elizabeth Brown Henley. Most people called her by her Cherokee name, Quatie. John and Quatie had six children—four boys and two girls. One of the girls died as a baby. John moved his family to a **plantation** in northern Georgia. There, he built a large two-story house. John quickly became one of the richest men in Georgia.

Elizabeth Brown Henley married John Ross around 1813.

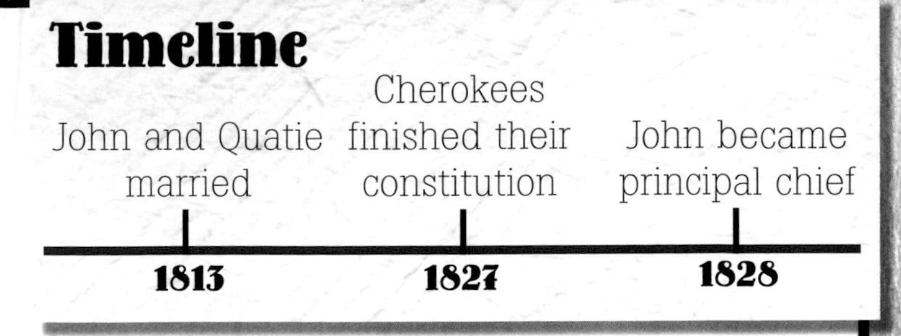

In 1822 Cherokee leaders began work on a **constitution** for their **nation.** They wanted to continue to be recognized as an independent nation. Cherokee leaders finished their constitution in 1827. In 1828 Cherokees elected John Ross to be their first principal chief. By this time, the Cherokee people had already lost almost all of their land. John wanted to make sure that his people would keep the rest of their land.

For a time, some Cherokees grew rich from money earned on their plantations. This mansion belonged to Chief James Vann.

Leading Through Hard Times

John's dream of keeping his people's **homeland** quickly fell apart. In 1832 leaders of the state of Georgia refused to accept the Cherokee people as their own **nation.** Georgia leaders decided to give Cherokee lands in Georgia to white **settlers.** John knew this was unfair. But he did not want to start a war. Instead he decided to take state leaders to court.

Magnetic Variation 5° East

SCALE OF 20 CHAINS TO AN INCH.

STATE OF GEORGIA.

THE above Plat is a representation of the Tract or Lot of Land, situate in the TWELFTH District, in the SECOND Section Cherokee County, containing One Hundred and Sixty Acres, and is known and distinguished in the plan of said District by the number One hundred & twelve (112)

SURVEYED on the 16th day of June 1832.

By J. Westmoreland B. F. Johnston Dist. Surveyor, W. Harris } C. C.

This is an 1832 map of Cherokee lands. Georgia leaders used maps like this one to divide up Cherokee lands for white settlers.

John's case made it to the United States Supreme Court. After hearing both sides, the Court decided that the state of Georgia could not take land from the Cherokees. John felt like he had won a major victory. But soon he saw that the court case had little effect on his people. Settlers continued to push the Cherokees off their lands. When the Cherokee people complained, no one did anything to help them.

Chief Justice John Marshall wrote the Supreme Court's decision in favor of the Cherokees.

During the next three years, the Cherokees split into two groups. One group believed the Cherokees should sell their lands and move west. This group was called the **Treaty** Party. The other group did not want to give up their homes. They were the National Party. John Ross led the National Party.

A Cherokee man named Major Ridge led the Treaty Party.

Timeline

Treaty of New Echota	Trail of Tears	Quatie died
1835	1838–1839	February 1, 1839

In 1835 Cherokee leaders met in Washington, D.C. There, members of the Treaty Party signed a treaty selling all Cherokee lands. John Ross felt **disappointed** as he traveled home. Overnight, John had lost his home, his cattle, and his fields. His people had lost their way of life. Three years later, the Cherokees made their journey west on the Trail of Tears.

This is the Treaty of New Echota. It shows the marks of the members of the Cherokee Treaty Party.

This is Major Ridge's mark. Many American Indians signed treaties with marks because they could not write in English.

On the Wrong Side

The trail ended in what is now the state of Oklahoma. John's group was the last to arrive. Families ran to greet each other. Other people cried over the deaths of their loved ones. John thought it was important to set up a new government. He wanted the government to **unite** all the Cherokee people. The Cherokee people elected John as Principal Chief of their new government. On September 6, 1839, the Cherokee **Nation** wrote a new **constitution.**

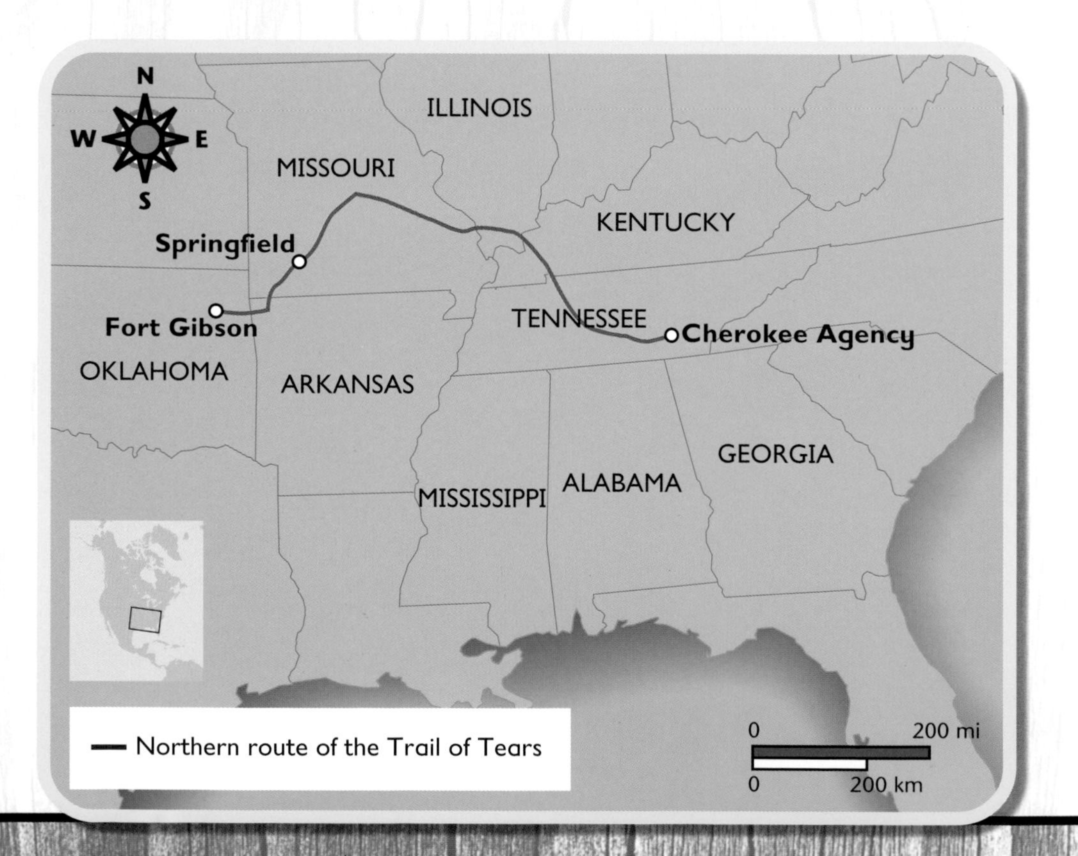

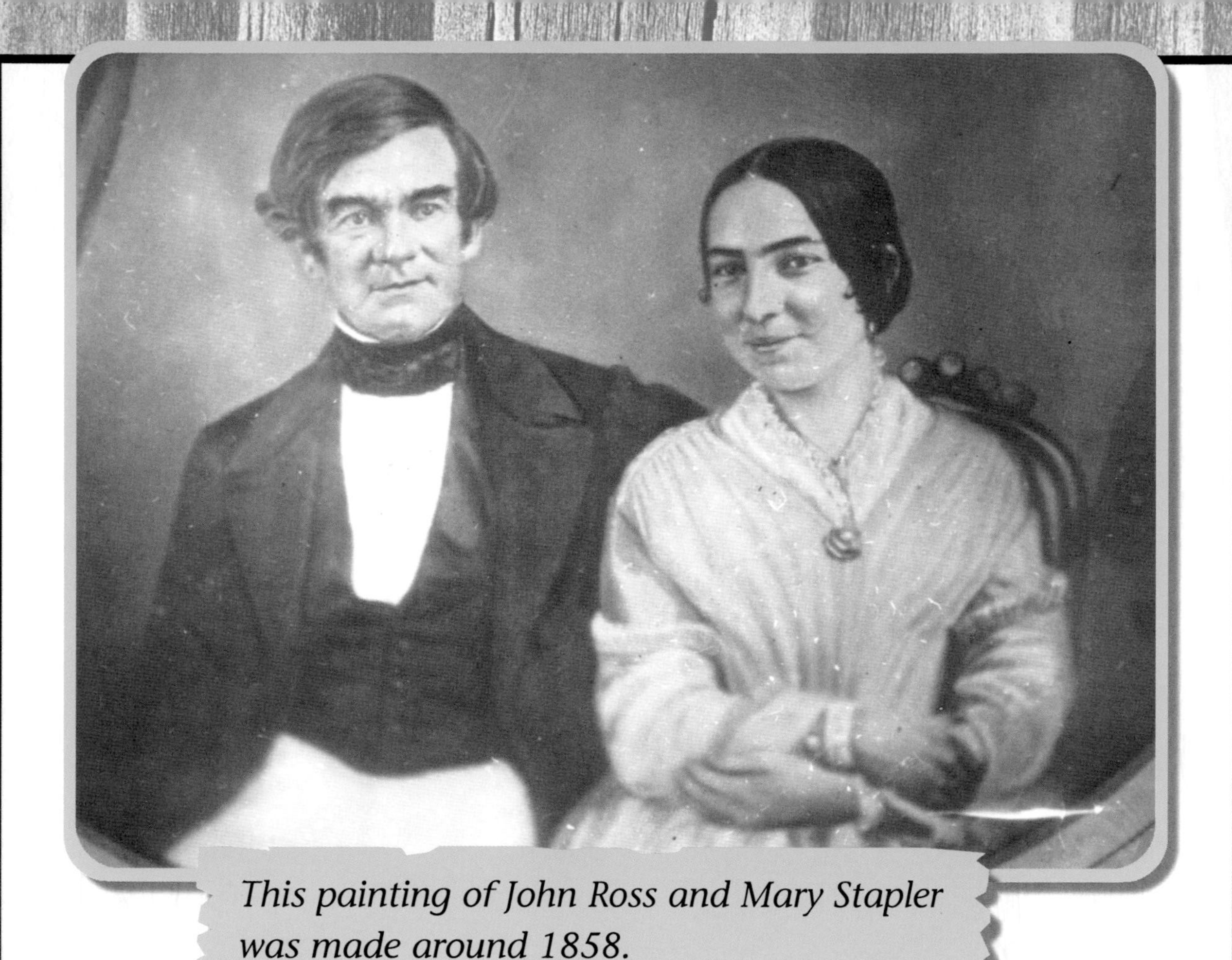

This painting of John Ross and Mary Stapler was made around 1858.

John tried to make the best of his new life. He married a woman named Mary Stapler. They built a home and called it Rose Cottage. Roses grew in their yard. John once again became a successful businessman. He owned a large **stable** for horses. John and Mary had two children together—Annie and John, Jr. For a while, life was good for the Cherokees. They built schools and businesses.

Some Cherokees fought with Texan soldiers against the North. Below is a painting of the Battle of Pea Ridge.

In 1861 the Civil War (1861–1865) began. At first, John Ross did not want the Cherokees to get involved. Later, some Cherokees joined the South's Confederate Army. Others joined the North's Union Army. But in 1862 the Union Army invaded the Cherokee **Nation.** John and his family were sent to Delaware. During the war, Rose Cottage was burned to the ground. In 1865 John returned to the Cherokee Nation.

Timeline

Annie Ross was born	John Jr. was born	Civil War	Mary died	John died
1845	**1847**	**1861–1865**	**July 20, 1865**	**August 1865**

On July 20, 1865, Mary died of a **lung disease.** John was very sad. After the war many United States leaders did not trust John. They opened Cherokee land to **settlers.** Suddenly the Cherokee Nation was split apart. John wanted to keep his people **united.** He met with government leaders to ask for help. After the meeting, John fell to the floor. A month later, he died.

This photograph shows Rose Cottage, John Ross's last home.

A Loyal Leader

John Ross served the Cherokee people for nearly 50 years. He helped them become and remain an independent **nation.** John never stopped fighting for his people's independence. But he chose to fight with words, not weapons. John led the Cherokees through some of the most difficult times in their history.

John Ross fought for the future children of the Cherokee Nation.

In 1870 the Cherokee Nation built a capitol for their government in Tahlequah, Oklahoma. Outside the capitol, they placed a monument in honor of John Ross. Today people celebrate John's life of hard work, **loyalty,** and **dedication** to his people.

John Ross was the principal chief of the Cherokees from 1828 to 1866. This monument to John Ross is outside the Cherokee capitol.

Glossary

buckskin deerskin leather made soft by tanning

ceremony event that celebrates a special occasion

constitution plan for government

dedication giving up what a person needs in order to work for an important cause or purpose

disappointed sad because something did not happen as hoped

elder older person, such as a grandparent, who is treated with respect

fast go without eating

herb plant used for food or medicine

heritage cultural identity

homeland place that a group of people comes from

immigrant person who comes to a new country to live there

landing place where boats can load and unload people or things onto land

loyalty being faithful to something a person believes in

lung disease sickness that affects the lungs

medicine man person with spiritual power

mocker person who makes fun of someone else

nation group of American Indians of the same tribe

plantation large farm

purify make clean

settler person who makes a home in a new place

stable building where horses are kept

trading post place where people trade things they have for things they need

treaty agreement between governments or groups of people

tutor person who helps one student learn

unite come together to do something

warrior person who fights in battles

More Books to Read

Burgan, Michael. *Trail of Tears.* Minneapolis: Compass Point Books, 2001.

Williams, Suzanne Morgan. *Cherokee Indians.* Chicago: Heinemann Library, 2003.

Todd, Anne M. *The Cherokee: An Independent Nation.* Minnetonka, Minn.: Capstone Press, 2002.

Index